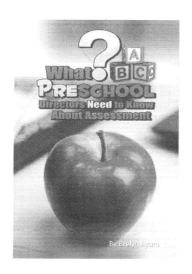

Evelyn Ayum
www.ebolocs@aol.com
www.ebolocs@gmail.com

Copyright ©2009 Evelyn Ayum
ISBN# 0-9665901-1-2

Contents

Foreword **7**
About this book **10**

A New Vision for Preschool Leadership 13
What Preschool Administrators need to Know About Leading 14
What Data is Needed For Improvement of Preschool Facilitates 15
Historically What Shaped Preschool Sites 17
What Collaboration is Essential for Preschool Administrators 18

What Preschool Teachers Should Know About Leadership 19
Preschool teachers learning to use assessment to guide student learning 19
Learning to look at information that affects the Learning Environment 20
Learning to use Playtime to assess Student-Learning 24
Opportunities for success 25

What Are Preschool Standards 25
How Preschool Teachers Interpret the Standards of Learning? 26

Assessing the Standards of Learning in the Preschool Classroom..................27
Interpreting the Results of Assessment to Make Decisions.................. 29

The Assessment Cycle..................29
The Process of Planning, Observing, Documenting, Evaluating and Implementing 31
Quality Components..................33

Assessment of the Preschool Classroom Environment..................33
Components of the Preschool Learning Environment..................35
Early Childhood Environment Rating Scale-Revised (ECERS-R)..................35
Space and Furnishing 36
Personal Care..................37
Language & Reasoning.................. 38
Activities.................. 39
Interactions.................. 40
Program Structure..................41
Parents and Staff..................42

Understanding the other Preschool Assessment Tools
What is the SELA?..44
What is the Purpose of the PCMI................................ 46
What is the SELLCA?...48
How to use Curriculum Implementation Tools? 49

Managing Assessment for the Purpose of Student Success................................. 50
Assessing Student Learning to Drive Instruction............51
How to evaluate students for the best results.................52
Collaboration among teachers to share student assessment...53

The Implications of Assessment for Preschool Administrators 55
How Data Empowers Preschool Administrators................55
Validating the Progress of Students and Staff..................56
Making Decisions...56

What To Do With The Information........ 56
Planning for Staff Development 57
Improving areas of Strengths and Weaknesses.................58
Collaboration with Stakeholders for Change....................59
Parent Involvement...60

Building a Team of Preschool Data Collectors..61
Creating Preschool Teacher Leaders................................63
Empowering Preschool Teachers with Data 63

Preschoolers at Risk 64-67
**Checklist for Preschool Administrators, Directors,
Teachers and Parents...68-70**
**Appropriate Assessment Practice for 3s, 4s, and
5 Year Olds...71-77**
Milestones for Preschooler 3s, 4s and 5 year Olds..........78-87
Getting Ready for Assessment Things to Think About.....88-89
Links to Important Websites for Directors.....................90-92
Books on Assessment..93-94
References..95
Appendix...96-108

Foreword

When you start a discussion about assessment with people the conversation turn towards who is going to be responsible for the information. Why are we collecting the information and where is it going to be stored for everyone to have access. Who is going to use the information and for what purpose? Preschool directors and administrators are surprised when they are asked about their assessment of their environment or the literacy assessment collected and compounded by their teachers. Many confess that they have never thought about the information collected because they never saw the use or the potential of the information.

However, it is mandatory that their preschool teachers assess students and their environment as an intricate part of their duties. The question is whether preschool teachers are using the information to improve their teaching or their preschool environment. In addition, how could preschool directors and administrators in many of the urban day care center settings improve the quality of their center by using the data collected from their preschool assessments?

As a Special Education Teacher for many years and a Resource Teacher Coordinator, I have committed myself to the idea that we need to know how to plan, assess and implement change if our students and families are going to improve the quality of their own lives. The challenge of the urban day care center is to be proactive in using the data collected and making use of the information to begin the process of change.

I like to thank the Preschool directors, administrators and teachers for helping me understand that in order to bring about change, we have to want to and we have to help those who understand and know about assessment to lead the way and show others how to use the data to bring about improvements. To become a "data leader" who presents the data, help analyze the data and implement changes based on the information.

About this book

This book is written to assist preschool directors understand the usefulness of preschool data and how easily it could help in their planning to implement changes in their preschool settings. In addition, it will educate preschool directors of the importance of using data and sharing it with preschool teachers to enhance their own teaching. Furthermore, it will help to implement needed changes of the preschool environment using the data collected. The process of analyzing data is clear once preschool directors and administrators understand what it entails. Planning and goal setting becomes easier.

In this book, I use many illustrations to demonstrate how the process of data collection can be managed over a period of time. It is my goal to show that this process never changes but the information can be valuable to improve the quality of preschool environments and maximize the learning achievement goals of their students. It is as simple as the steps towards becoming a "data leader." Each step reveals and explains the process as clearly as possible.

Step 1. Data collection is the information gathered from teachers about their students and their environment.

Step 2. Analyzing the data collected to improve the quality of the environment and student achievement.

Step 3. Implementation of the information learned from the data collected to make decisions that are cost effective, beneficial for all stakeholders at the center and create the staff development necessary to empower the school staff, students and their families.

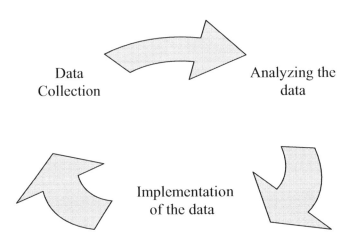

Figure 1

A New Vision for Preschool Leadership

Preschool leadership is on the move and is constantly changing, as the need for technology is increases so is what we say and do with it. Our young children are moving rapidly through the information age. With smarter technology and the use of the internet and what it has to offer. Preschool leadership must also change and be able to prepare our young learners. A new vision of leadership must take place--one that requires leadership to implement change through the use of data. It is important for preschool directors to seek out new and exciting technology to enhance and educate preschool teachers and families. By leading by example, preschool directors examine the data teachers collect work samples on students; discuss the implications the results show and analyze how to proceed to make necessary changes.

What preschool administrators need to know in order to lead the process of data collection is the following information:

- Use data on a daily basis
- Train staff to use data
- Establish a routine in centers or district schools where data is used.
- Make the data accessible to both teachers and other staff members.
- Collect the data and celebrate its achievement
- Apply for accreditations by documenting the successful data of preschool teachers.
- Examine data on an on-going basis in order to set goals and implement changes

What Data Tools Preschool Directors Need:

When we have the data in hand, we have a powerful tool.

E.J.

The tools that preschool directors need when making decisions about their preschool classroom environment and academic curriculum are the following:

➢ Directors need to have access to past data and review what areas need strengthening.
➢ Have a good understanding of the curriculum that teachers are using and have periodic discussions with other administrators, teachers and stakeholders about the data
➢ Review how preschool teachers are planning and what expectations are appropriately being planned for young learners
➢ Make sure that they have a copy of all the necessary books: curriculum guide, preschool expectations, the Environmental Rating Scales and a developmental Continuum that shows where individual children at each stage of development are.

- Monitor data on a routine bases so that all staff members understand your goals
- Create a timeline for continued observation of data
- Have assessment on-hand and accessible when it's needed to refer to.
- Plan staff development using tools of assessment.

It is important that Directors are knowledgeable about the data that is being gathered to monitor trends and evaluate their programs. They must be accountable for how we educate our young learners. The purpose is to examine the data and show how we can better serve our students and identify those students for health and special services. To help our parents become educated about their early learners and provide them with the strategies and support they need.

Historically What Shaped Preschool Sites

What shaped preschools today I believe were the Head Start program. Head Start began in 1965 and was a program started by the United States Department of Health and Human Services. The Head Start program was created for poor children. What was discovered was that children who attended the Head Start program did better than those who didn't.

According to Datta (Datta, 1976 & Lee et al.,1990) who summarized 31 studies, the Head Start program showed immediate improvement in the IQ scores of participating children, though after beginning school, the non-participants were able to narrow the difference. Children who attended Head Start are, relative to their siblings who did not, significantly more likely to complete high school, attend college, and possibly have higher earnings in their early twenties. They are less likely to have been booked or charged with a crime.[11] Head Start is associated with large and significant gains in test scores. Head Start significantly reduces the probability that a child will repeat a grade.[1]

What Collaboration is Essential for Preschool Administrators

The collaboration that is essential for preschool administrators when looking at data is for them to collaborate with members of their school society so they can use the data in addition to the following:

- Collect the data from teachers about their students
- Analyze the data and reflect on the information
- Get teachers perspective of the data
- Decide on what to do with the information
- Show the information in clear form where everyone will understand
- Share the information with those stakeholders who will use it
- Help students and their parents use the data to improve weaknesses

What Preschool Teachers Should Know About Leadership

Preschool teachers need to know that leadership takes different forms and one of the things that they need to do is understand the data they collect on their preschool students. With this information, they will be better able to prepare for students who are having difficulties and those who aren't. Teachers would be able to use concrete information to improve instruction. When teachers use data, they are using factual information about what is going on in their classroom and using it to improve students learning. Teachers who become teacher leaders want to see results and want to see their students succeed.

Preschool teachers learning to use assessment to guide student learning

Preschool administrators who are knowledgeable about assessment can help preschool teachers look more closely at assessment by showing them the usefulness that the data has to offer. For example, if directors and teachers understand their curriculum, they can plan more effectively and assess failing students to find appropriate strategies for them. Using data to assess student learning, helps teachers create meaningful lessons that support student learning by:

- Lesson planning according to student data
- Preparing small group instruction to support student learning
- Defining where the problems are in order to make changes
- Setting goals for students that help them become successful
- Continuing to improve all aspects of learning for preschool students and their families by involving parents as much as possible in children's education.

Learning to look at information that affects the learning environment

The learning environment is where preschoolers do their best learning. They are acting on their learning in the following learning areas:

1. **Circle time Area:** Teachers and students gather together to discuss what's going to happen during the day. Teachers

share their plans with students, sing songs, tell stories and show interesting objects.

2. **Dramatic Play Area:** Preschoolers pretend to be chefs in a kitchen, shop owners, bakers, shoe makers etc. They have an opportunity to communicate with each other and learn about the various careers adult can have just by pretending to be that person.

3. **Toy and Games Area:** Students have an opportunity to use their skills at counting, connecting objects, building towers, grouping similar things and piecing together puzzles. They learn social behavior with their peers in an effort to communicate and expand their language.

4. **Sand and Water Area:** In this area, preschoolers make discoveries with sand and water. Use tools to shovel sand, make sand castles, model objects in the sand, find and bury objects in the sand.

5. **Discovery Area:** Preschoolers have an opportunity to look at objects under a microscope, examine rocks, read dinosaur books, observe small animals, create and take care of plants.

6. **Block Area:** Here preschoolers get to use their imagination to build and replicate buildings that they see in everyday life. They use their natural senses to measure, count, assess and share information about various shapes and sizes.

7. **Computer area:** In the computer area, teachers help preschoolers—count numbers, match objects, match upper and lowercase letters, differentiate sounds, draw pictures, write and read messages and play games.

8. **Art Area:** In the area art, students have an opportunity to express themselves through painting pictures. Preschoolers test their abilities to replicate what they see in the real world. They paint pictures about fictional characters, their families and many other people, places and things that affect their world.

9. **Music Area:** Making music is a natural activity for preschoolers. They like to pretend to play a musical instrument in this area and

sing songs that they have heard. With teachers facilitating, preschoolers can communicate and draw on their ability to create authentic sounds that they create.

10. **Library Area:** The library area introduces preschoolers to a wealth of great books both fictional and non-fictional. Many preschoolers use puppets and other storytelling objects to retell stories and act out story characters. Storytelling is important in encouraging preschoolers to enjoy reading. Most preschool teachers read to preschoolers at least twice daily. It is important to assess students learning while students are in the midst of their learning. Thereby, teachers can take actual and factual notes of what their preschoolers are doing. Assessment of students abilities while they are engaged in play is one-way teachers can make decisions on how to plan lessons.

Learning to Use Playtime to Assess Student-Learning

Many preschooler teachers are just beginning to understand the importance of using data to plan what goes on in the learning areas that assess student learning. Assessment is a tool that helps teachers to plan lessons and appropriate activities for young learners. As teachers observe students in each area, they can prepare individualized lessons to improve student learning. In addition, the information on students can inform a parent of their child's social development. It helps teachers examine the developmental levels of their students. The developmental continuum helps preschool teachers with what to look for in relationship to student development.

The preschool developmental continuum is one of the preschool development tools that have successfully addressed what and how to look at child development. The developmental continuum assessment addresses the following data: physical, social/emotional, cognitive, language, reading and writing development. Preschool teachers use their observational and anecdotal notes on students to make decisions about student learning and how to help a student progress on the continuum

Opportunities for success

If preschool directors and administrators would use the information collected effectively, the data could consistently prove to be very useful in making predictions about particular students and groups of children at their centers. In addition, the use of statistical data to make decisions about the academic progress of preschoolers is far removed because most preschool directors and administrator have not been taught that preschool data is relevant. However, today, a move towards analyzing specific information that can shape the very foundation of a preschool center is important in determining whether a center fails or succeeds.

What Are Preschool Standards

The preschool standards are those standards that directors, administrators and teachers use as benchmarks to assess what they teach preschoolers. These standards measure the behaviors and conditions of what teachers use to teach lessons. The standards are an important tool that address the purpose of why teachers teach a certain concept or skill.

How Preschool Teachers Interpret the Standards of Learning

Preschool teachers interpret the standards of learning by how their children are learning to process the skills they are learning. There are various concepts in reading, writing, math, science, social and emotional, physical, social studies and technology that preschoolers need to learn. It is important for preschool directors and teachers to understand how and what should be taught to preschooler. Preschoolers have to be taught to think, create, recall, remember and understand what they are learning--in order to be productive learners who can act on their learning and create authentic work a that a teacher can assess. In order for this to happen, teachers have to be rigorous in how they preparing their lessons and carefully deciding what to teach.

Assessing the Standards of Learning in the Preschool Classroom

As preschool directors approach analyzing the preschool classroom, they have to look at the standards in relationship to the environment. It is important to focus on the ten interest areas I previously spoke about. What children are doing in the interest areas and what teachers have prepared for them can ultimately affect how they are learning.

The environment must be accessible in every way to students. Preschoolers have to act on their learning in a positive way to assure success. There are learning outcomes that all preschoolers must know and learn in order to assure success in school.

The standards, along with the preschool curriculum are what drive the instruction. Assessment is the means by which preschool teachers look closely at student strengths and weaknesses and decide how to move students progressively. The figure below illustrates the direction or course teachers should follow when assessing the learning environment and what directors need to know in order to assess teachers and students.

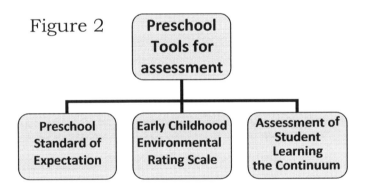

Figure 2

Interpreting the Results of Assessment to Make Decisions

Interpreting the results of your assessment overall is being able to have access to the data in a timely fashion in order to make the necessary decisions that are needed to move the center along. Directors have to become data leaders in order to understand the direction that a center is going and help teachers assess what they are doing. Assessment is a collaborative effort and must be a discussion as such, among professionals who come together to decide the steps to take in order to help young learners achieve their goals.

The Assessment Cycle

The assessment cycle has to be practiced and internalized before directors can understand the process of assessment as discussed earlier. The first step is to **plan** who is to be part of the assessment cycle. The second step is to **observe** how the process is working. That is what teachers are doing and how students are behaving. The third step is **documenting** and measuring what developmentally students are learning by the standards in which learning outcomes are measured. Directors need to know what these standards of measurements are and how teachers are using them to plan and observe students. The fourth step in **evaluating** these steps requires that directors and teachers look at all the data at hand and plan instruction that is meaningful and useful to improve student learning. The idea is assessment for learning in order for preschoolers to improve their skills. Finally, after examining all the data collected and making the necessary decisions for students, the fifth step is **implementation.** How directors influence teachers to implement the changes needed and use the information that the data shows. Later in this book we will look at an Early Childhood Rating Score assessment and analyze what changes should be made to that preschool environment.

The Process of Planning, Observing, Documenting, Evaluating and Implementing

The process of assessment was discussed above to illustrate what steps have to be taken in making the learning stakes necessary to improve the preschool center and what preschool students are learning. The figure below illustrates the targeted goal at a center which is always student achievement. The challenge of all preschool directors is to disaggregate the data so that teachers, parents and those stakeholders (i.e., directors, teachers, parents, nurses, doctors and community activist) who are interested in the results to understand what's at stake. In addition, define what direction should be implemented to improve student's achievement.

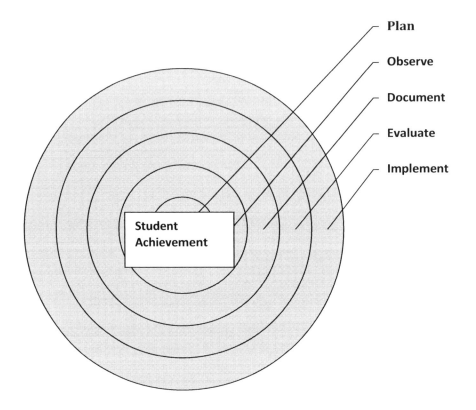

Figure 3

Quality Components

The quality component of the preschool environment is what teachers teach children. Lesson plans should be relevant and meaningful to the preschooler's development as it relates to what he/she is learning in the preschool classroom. The instructional focus must be clear before achievable goals can be. The director has to also be an instructional leader who understands how to inform teachers as they formulate timelines as to what concepts and skills they teach students. This too requires important planning, observing, measuring, evaluating and implementing student assessment which is a major element in the assessment process.

Assessment of the Preschool Classroom Environment

Assessment of the preschool classroom environment is important because it helps teachers assess how children are interacting and using the classroom environment.

Preschoolers need to be familiar with where they can hang their coats, get their blankets and other toys and where to nap. It empowers preschoolers when they know their environment is free of distractions. Teachers should be knowledgeable about the layout of their room and understand how pictures and labels reinforce how preschooler access items on the shelves and locate items in the room. Preschoolers need to be able to know who is here today and who is out. In addition, preschoolers need to know where in the room is their favorite project

Preschoolers need to have a sense of belonging. Teachers should make it their business to know about where each child comes from and document and post students' heritage in a thoughtful manner. When preschoolers see their native flags, they instantly bond to the environment that they are placed.

Components of Preschool Learning Environments

The Components of the Preschool Learning Environment consists of several areas. These areas are essential to how well preschoolers learn.

Early Childhood Environment Rating Scale-Revised (ECERS-R)

The Early Childhood Environment Rating Scale measure from 1 to 7 on the scale and 7 is the highest and 1 is the lowest. After the observation or assessment an action plan is created to remedy the weaker areas.

Space and Furnishing: There are eight items that are measured. You can review them on the graph below.

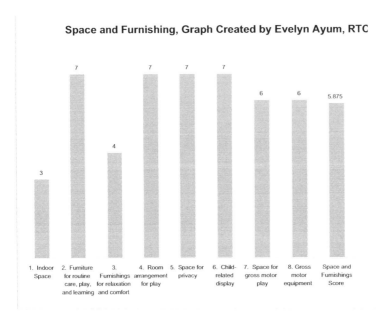

Indoor space is one of the items that examines if preschooler have enough space.

Furniture for routine: examines the height of tables and chairs; if they are safe and steady enough for preschoolers.

Furnishings for relaxation: examines how comfortable preschoolers are; do they have the necessary softness for them to be comfortable.

Personal Care

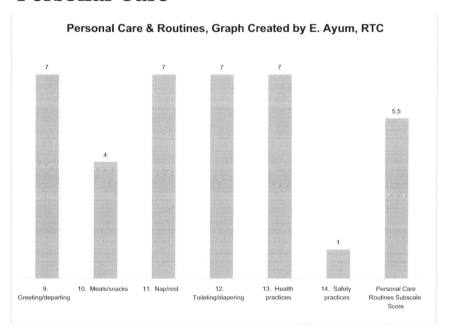

There are several areas that are examined here: greeting and departing of students and their family members. How meals and snacks are handled and are children involved in the process. Toileting and diapering; do children understand how to wash their hand and flush the toilet. Do teachers follow health practices and do they keep their environment safe for young children?

Language & Reasoning

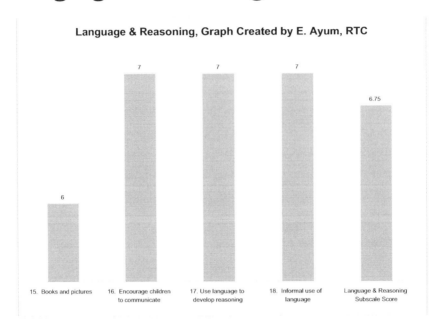

Language and reasoning addresses how books and other literacy materials are being use in the preschool classroom. How these materials encourage children to write read and express themselves. In addition, how teachers and other staff members encourage children to express themselves both formally and informally. The ECERS is a great instrument for directors to assess their staff in these areas and help in planning staff development activities that are meaningful for teachers.

Activities

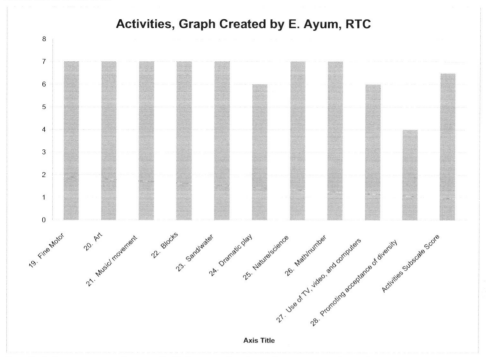

Activities are what children do in the preschool environment; how they interact with the supplies in their environment and do they have enough items to play without fighting over them. The examiner looks at the labeling and the accessibility; how preschoolers are able to get these items off the shelves and do they know how to put them back. These are the ten interest areas spoken about earlier.

Interactions

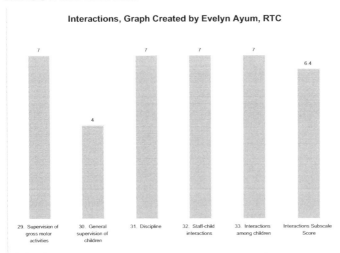

The interactions scale examines how successful teachers and assistants are at engaging students in conversations. Teachers are expected to have at least five exchanges with students during conversations with them. Teacher ask students open-ended questions about their play hoping to get a better understanding of what they are thinking and what interests them. The dialogue between students and staff is measured on the ECERS assessment. It gives the observer a clear picture of what takes place on an occasion where there is no observation. By assessing teacher behavior while they are interacting with students, the director has some insight on how to affect change.

Program Structure

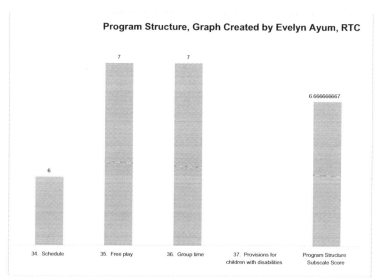

The program structure is how preschool directors run their program. This is basically the schedule. It is important when the teacher, students and parents understand the daily schedule in a preschool setting. For children, it gives them a sense of familiarity with their day. They know when its time for routine activities such as playtime, outdoor time, lunchtime and snack time. When children understand the schedule of the day they feel safe and secure.

Parents and Staff

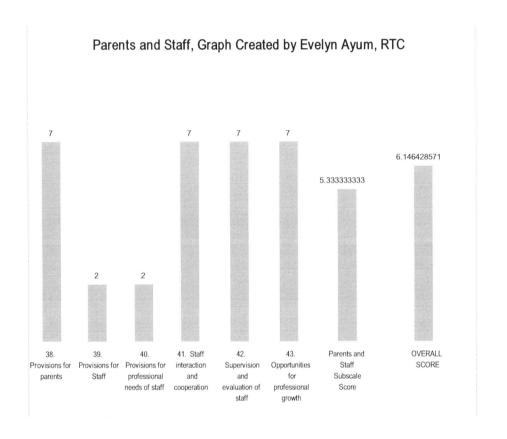

Parents and family involvement is what keeps parents and other family members abreast of the lastest activities of the preschool program. Parents know when to expect certain things such as when there are school closings, special events, trips and emergency situations. Provisions for parents and staff are just as important so parents can feel a sense of belonging with the preschool program. Staff involvement is also another important aspect of preschool life. It is just as important for a staff member to feel that he or she is relevant to the preschool program. They need to know that they are making a difference in the lives of preschool children and their families. Directors should make staff members feel that they are an intergral part of the program and the school they should assure teachers that they are secure in their jobs. Teachers need to know that the director has a goal or vision in mine for the school he/she should employ many ways to help teachers understand that there is a direction that the school is going.

    The director plans professional development opportunities to help teachers improve their practice and gain insight into the best practices for preschoolers. It is the leadership of the director that encourages and support teachers throughout the day; and helping them discover ways to improve students learning and academic success.

Understanding the other Preschool Assessment Tools

What is the SELA?

The Support of Early Literacy Assessment addresses what to look for in a literacy rich environment. For instance, the use of print in the environment and whether it serves a purpose. In addition, does the classroom have an inviting place for children to look at books and are there a wide variety. Are there writing materials available and do children have easy access to them. Do children have a variety of props for pretend play that they can interact with? The SELA also examines the following categories listed on the next page.

TEACHER
OBSERVER

SELA
THE LITERATE ENVIRONMENT
1. PRINT IN ENVIRONMENT FOR PURPOSE
2. CREATING INVITING PLACES TO LOOK AT BOOKS
3. INVITING INTEREST IN A WIDE VARIETY OF BOOKS
4. WRITING MATERIALS AVAILABLE & EASY FOR CHILDREN TO USE
5. VARIETY OF LITERACY ITEMS & PROPS USED IN PRETEND AREA

AVERAGE

LANGUAGE DEVELOPMENT
6. ENCOURAGE USE & EXTEND ORAL LANGUAGE
7. INTRODUCE NEW WORDS, CONCEPTS, & LINGUISTIC STRUCTURES
8. PROMOTE ORAL LANG DEV & BUILD KNOWLEDGE
9. LANGUAGE/KNOWLEDGE/LOVE BOOK READING

AVERAGE

KNOWLEDGE OF PRINT/BOOK CONCEPTS
10. FUNCTIONS/FEATURES OF PRINT

AVERAGE

PHONOLIGICAL AWARENESS
11. ATTENTION TO SOUNDS

AVERAGE

LETTERS AND WORDS
12. RECOGNIZE LETTERS
13. INTEREST IN WRITING

AVERAGE

PARENT INVOLVEMENT
14. HOME-BASED SUPPORT
15. ACTIVITIES AND SUPPORTS

AVERAGE

BILINGUAL/NON-ENGLISH
20. NATIVE LANGUAGE

AVERAGE
CLASSROOM AVERAGE
PROGRAM AVERAGE

What is the Purpose of the PCMI?

The Preschool Children Math Instrument analyzes the necessary components of a quality math program. The PCMI is an assessment tool that examines what math tools and used in a preschool classroom. The PCMI outlines the types of games, puzzles, counters that are being used in a quality preschool math classroom. The instrument assesses the content areas of math that are important to preschoolers such as numbers and numeration, geometry and spatial sense, logical thinking and data collection.

The PCMI addresses ways that teachers are presenting math activities to students; the types of math supplies it addresses how teachers engage students during math. In addition, the instrument assesses the math language of students and the environment and really pinpoints areas where math ideas are not taking place. It is important for a teacher to talk about math throughout the day with students. Below are the areas of the PCMI that are addressed.

Observer Name:
PCMI
Materials
1. Materials for counting, comparing, estimating, and recognizing numbers
2. Materials for measuring and comparing amount
3. Materials for classifying and seriating
4. Materials for geometry and spatial positions/ relations
Interactions/Activities
5. Teachers encourage one-to-one correspondence
6. Teachers encourage children to count/write numbers for a purpose
7. Teachers encourage children to estimate and compare numbers
8. Teachers encourage mathematical terminology and reflection
9. Teachers encourage children to measure and compare amounts
10. Teachers encourage children to classify and seriate
11. Teachers encourage concepts of geometry and spatial positions

What is the SELLCA?

The Support for English Language Learner Child Assessment is another tool that directors need to familiarize themselves with. This instrument assesses the types of books and materials that teachers are using with bilingual students. The SELLCA is important because it addresses the needs of bilingual students in the preschool environment.

When using the SELLCA in the proper way, it can assist directors and teachers on how to best address the behavior and needs of bilingual students and their families. It is important to note that directors can obtain the PCMI, SELA and SELLCA from their resource teacher coordinator.

How to use Curriculum Implementation Tools?

For instance, the Creative Curriculum Implementation tool helps preschool directors understand the searches to building a quality program –what supplies are needed and what teachers should do to improve their environment and interaction with children. This tool profiles and highlights the following items:

Physical environment
Interest area materials, furnishings, equipment displays.

The structure of the day daily schedule and routines, large and small group time, choice time, transitions and weekly plans

Teacher-child interactions building relationships, guiding children's behavior, general strategies, literacy, mathematics, science, social studies, the arts, technology, studies.

Assessment observation and documentation, analyzing and evaluating children's progress and planning for individuals and groups and

Family Involvement the interactions and collaborations with family members in the community.

Finally there are also interview questions that the director, principal or administrator can ask the teacher.

Managing Assessment for the Purpose of Student Success

Now that you have a familiar understanding what is needed to address assessment? What are the instruments involved? What do you do with them? Once you have all the necessary assessments completed how do you handle all this information? I suggest that preschool directors take some time to read all the data and digest and plan for the next steps. You want to be able to know how to process the information and share the information with the people that need it. It is important to set timelines to address your plan of action. Know the areas that you can address immediately and strive to do so for immediate implementation. When you address assessment with teachers immediately, they'll have a clear idea of your expectations. Your staff begins to understand what is important to you and will know that you too look at assessment.

Assessing Student Learning to Drive Instruction

Student learning is the ultimate goal of any preschool director. You want to make sure that young learners are getting the best out of your preschool program. You want to have concrete examples of student achievement and you want teachers to work with students from where they are. When teachers assess student learning, they have a guide as to how they are going to instruct their lessons with students. Teachers begin to create meaningful and purposeful lessons that improve student learning and assist in the student's growth and development. One of the ways that teachers can plan instruction is by using the Preschool Standards that address what's appropriate to teach and how to teach it.

The Preschool Standards have been updated and directors can go online and download the new standards from the Department of Education website. Directors should familiarize themselves with what the standard says in accordance with the various goals and expectations outlined in this booklet. The preschool expectations are essential for both teachers and preschool directors.

How to evaluate students for the best results

The best way to evaluate students is by observing their behavior; what they are doing and saying. Teachers have many ways to assess student learning and one of them is to take anecdotal notes while children are conversing and learning alongside their peers. There have been many early learning behaviors that have been discovered as a result of watching children in their natural setting. Parents watch their children for many signs such as whether they are functioning the way that most babies or preschooler at certain ages do. Piaget the leading theorist on child watching has made several discoveries about children and their physical and cognitive development. Clearly observation of children can improve and help teachers make decisions that improve student learning and create meaningful lessons and activities for young learners.

Collaboration among teachers to share student assessment

Directors need to stay current as to the many ideas out there that affect student learning and improve teacher practice. It is important that teachers collaborate with each other and share success with each other as to what worked and did not work in their classroom. When teachers share assessment with each other, they build stronger networks with colleagues that help improve student achievement. Teachers brainstorm lessons and activities that seem to work with students. They share ideas that help them become more reflective and purposeful in their planning.
Teachers should have an opportunity to digest their own assessment information to make changes. There are great moments and exciting ideas that are associated with how teachers address assessment and share

their thinking. It is the ability of teachers who have a knowledge base about what is developmentally appropriate for learners in their earlier years.

Directors have to use many methods of leadership to achieve greater results and lead with conviction and a purpose, which is to improve student achievement. The ultimate goal is for directors and administrators to understand the types of assessment that guide them toward continuous improvements to student learning. There has to be an established value system that mimics successful results and which is shared by those who have direct effect on student learning. Over the years, I have witness many ineffective administrators who didn't know how to appropriately and continuously use data as an ongoing process to inform and promote those areas that needed changing.

The Implications of Assessment for Preschool Administrators

The implications of assessment for preschool administrators are invaluable and immeasurable. Mainly it is the administrator's duty to make sure that the school environment is intact; that learning is taking place no matter what area of the classroom student are placed and that students have the necessary supplies that are needed.
Hence, teachers also have to be conscious of where they are whether it's in a small or large classroom environment. The only way you are going to effect higher student achievement is through the teacher and his or her actions in the classroom.

How Data Empowers Preschool Administrators?

When Preschool administrators understand data it empowers them to understand how to improve their school and make it more successful. By gathering appropriate information that allows them to make strategic decisions about workshops that improve teachers' skills and improve student achievement. Using the assessment data, teachers are able to specifically pinpoint areas of weaknesses and create meaningful lessons that improve instructions for students. When preschool administrators understand data, they can continue to make decisions that provide teachers and students with the support they need to make decisions that support young children development.

Validating the Progress of Students and Staff Making Decisions:
What To Do With The Information

Often, preschool teachers are the ones who report information about students to parents and they are also the ones who collect and document what preschoolers are learning and how they are doing. They have periodic meetings with parents to share the information. Preschool teachers try to help parents with understanding how their child/children are doing in the preschool classroom. Teachers make decisions on how to improve students' learning and they also provide parents with specific strategies to help students with learning or behavior disabilities.

Planning for Staff Development

Preschool administrators are in a unique position to have access to a lot of data: curriculum information and ideas, assessment evaluation of the preschool environment, testing and attendance. The information that is collected from the above is instrumental in helping to create meaning staff development that improve and enhance instruction.

Staff development is important when the presenter delivers information that help teachers to "think outside the box" and challenge them to use new ideas that support and improve student achievement.

Improving areas of Strengths and Weaknesses

Preschool directors can use assessment information to determine how to make adjustments to the curriculum, and have discussion with staff members about lesson plan ideas and how to make learning for preschoolers' relevant to their own lives. When assessment is used appropriately, teachers, students and parents benefit. The data that's used helps to improve and strengthen weaknesses--if the information is studied and reflective conversation that takes place between the stakeholders who can use the information to set meaningful goals and improve student achievement.

Teachers can develop topics of studies that preschoolers are interested in and meaningful learning takes place. Teachers are then able to differentiate instruction based on the needs of students. Directors will be able to help teachers with ideas on how to develop instruction that meet students at their level. Preschoolers are developing early learning skills in reading and writing that happens in the moment. Authentic learning takes place all the time when young children are realistically involved in their learning—when they are actively engaged.

Collaboration with Stakeholders for Change

The collaboration that directors create is long lasting and benefits young learners and their parents, teachers and the community. It is this meaningful collaboration that helps children progress also with their parents. In addition, meaningful relationships that take place in the school environment helps to shape the kind of activities that take place in school.

Many directors often ignore the powerful relationship that parents contribute to a school environment. In the book, "Dealing With Angry Parent," the author says, "it's the parents that bring balance to a school environment and encourage learning that stimulates excitement and creates a warm place for students. And when the relationship with teachers and parents are encouraged the school evolves into a more inviting place for learning."

Parent Involvement

Pitt the authority on parent involvement once remarked, "A school without a parent is a house without a guardian." Parents and teachers are true guardians of children learning. They are the ones that support the development of children by providing them with the nurturing they need to be excited about learning. Many parents today are sometimes working two and three jobs to support their families and some work long hours.

Often, young children are left for long hours in school and it's sometimes the teachers and other support staff that nurture students. In this regard, parents have to really stay closely involved with the school and their child's education. They have to remain diligent and stay connected with the school and teachers. It is the director's job to see that parents are involved at the very top of the agenda of what their school is all about. The vision the preschool center is to have clear ideas about on how parents can support a school spirit.

Building a Team of Preschool Data Collectors

The goal of a preschool director is to try to create an atmosphere in the school where shared responsibility is taking place. One of the ways in which the director can contribute to the vision of the school in relationship to data is to encourage teachers to use it. It is necessary for teachers and other members of the school "buy into" the idea that data collection and analysis is useful to improve student's skills.

The director can reinforce how teachers and other members use data; build teams of data collectors who examine data; and set goals. Here are some ideas on how to build your team of data collectors:

- Establish times during the day or week when teachers and other staff members can review and analyze data.
- Help teachers create times during the day to help make decisions around data.
- Monitor the progress that your teams are making.
- Celebrate success so that it is meaningful and useful to teachers and other staff members.
- Set goals for when improvements will be met and provide clear strategies and follow through practices that support teachers and students.
- Involve parents as much as possible in your decision-making.

Creating Preschool Teacher Leaders

When you create preschool teacher leaders, the school is on the path of change. It takes many people who can plan what can happen when children are learning and teachers are confident about what they are teaching. There are many tools that teachers use in order to make decisions and one of them is lesson plan and how data affects their decision on what to teach. When teachers are highly motivated by what children learn, spends a significant amount of time on lesson planning and creating an authentic classroom environment that is conducive to learning.
Directors need to know and pinpoint those teacher leaders and encourage them to share their unique abilities with the whole school.

Empowering Preschool Teachers with Data

Directors should help teachers manage the data and check in from time to time to see that the information is up-to-date. This means that they should do the following:

- Help teachers to reflect on the information that they collect on students.
- Support teachers with meaningful strategies and workshops that improve their learning.
- Think of technological software that makes collection easier.
- Schedule times for meeting with teachers and stakeholders who can improve the quality of assessment.
- Embrace parental support and help parents to understand how they can help their children at home.
- Connect with outside organizations that help support your vision for the future.

Preschoolers at Risk: Special Education Services

Most directors are confused about how to provide support for children who are in need of additional skills. It is important for they to familiarize themselves with individual reading, writing and speaking specialists who understand child development. The following is suggested for directors to enhance their understanding of preschoolers who are at risk of special education services.

- Directors should meet with their resource teachers and social workers to try and get the best possible solutions to help preschoolers
- Collaborate with outside service providers who understand the best practice and strategies to meet student needs.

- Schedule meetings with parents and other stakeholders that support children learning and behavioral development.
- Directors should create a protocol that deals with children in need of special education support—reading, writing and speaking.
- Connect with hospitals and other institutions.
- Monitor the successes of children and families and try to replicate it.

- Directors have to understand that early interventions are important for young learners.

In the appendix of this book, I have listed several places to find preschool intervention support. Here are some steps to getting referral in a timely manner:

1. *The teacher should have documented what are the student's strengths and weaknesses.*

2. *The teacher should notify the parents as to what is going on with his or her child.*

3. *Work samples of the student's work-- reading, writing and language.*

4. *The preschool intervention resource team should give strategies to the teacher and the teacher should note any progress made.*

5. *Meetings should be set up where the teacher, school nurse, intervention team*

and other members are consulting on the child.

The above ideas are a good place to start when a preschool director needs to consult on the process of referring a child when he or she has a learning or behavior disability.

Assessment Checklist for the Preschool Directors and Teachers

Schedule time to review assessment materials.	Set goals which are achievable surrounding assessments.
Monitor the progress of students using assessment information.	Collaborate with stakeholders and report findings of assessment.
Have meeting with teachers to analyze assessment.	Celebrate assessment successes and challenge weaknesses.
Report assessment information to Parent in a timely fashion.	Use assessment to track students with specific learning difficulty.
Document students' learning and have a reasonable collect period.	Schedule assessment meetings with learning specialist.
Plan meaningful instruction that is reflective of the assessment.	Design meaningful workshops on how to analyze assessment.
Differentiate instructions for all learners based on students' assessment.	Connect with other outside organizations to monitor and analyze assessment.

I am sure that there are other suggestions that many directors use to get ready to assess students' information. It is important that you analyze the assessment information that is collected. Directors have to take the lead and demonstrate to teachers that assessment is going to drive instruction and improve the performance of students.

In addition, teachers have to be convinced that someone is actually using assessment materials. So often I hear teachers complain that they collect all types of assessment information and no one besides them looks at the information or make suggestions as to what they are documenting.
Nevertheless, teachers do it because they are told to do so by principals, directors or their direct supervisor.

Many teachers admit they don't really look at the information because they know what their individual children can do. However, it is up to the principal, directors and administrators to forge the way and make a strong case that assessment is purposeful and meaningful to understanding children learning and for planning lessons that will yield results.

Appropriate Assessment Practice for 3s, 4s and 5 Years Old

There are purposeful activities that teachers can create for 3s, 4s and 5 years olds to make their experiences in school more successful both physically, cognitively, socially and intellectually. Examining each child's developmental stage and designing lessons that are appropriate is one way to create meaningful activities.

When teachers take anecdotal records of individual children, they are looking at the different growth patterns of children and using the curriculum and those interactions to develop activities based on their developmental ability levels and then designing lessons that are appropriate.

Secondly, when assessing children, the emphasis should be placed on the child's self-esteem and improving their self-esteem to communicate, complete tasks and to motivate the child to do more. Teachers have to intentionally prepare the preschool environment to get the ultimate learning behavior from students.

Materials have to be available to teach preschooler how to use them in an appropriate way. For instance, there should be at least 300 blocks in the block area for preschoolers to be able to challenge them to build complex structures. Teachers can model types of structures, discuss the names of the various blocks and relate to other geometry shapes and three-dimensional materials for exploration.

Children learn through active play in the various interest areas in the preschool classroom and it's the teacher's responsibility to prepare the areas in the classroom to support student learning.

In addition, children work should be authentically documented to really assess where individual children's levels are. The concrete materials used in the classroom with children can inform you on types of levels of equipment and materials teachers can use to assess student learning. It is important for teachers to intentionally plan small group activities with materials that are appropriate for the lessons that they are trying to teach. One way to do this is, for teachers to test their lessons on themselves--put themselves in the child's place—think of the possible errors they think would occur based on what they observe on a daily basis with preschoolers. Lessons and activities for preschoolers should be based on relevant experiences that students deal with on a daily basis: playing outdoors, communicating with family members, going to a grocery, a flower shop, a fish market or a bakery. Students need to learn where they live and what numbers to call when they need help. They can learn how to prepare simple meals and where to look on a cereal box in addition, to reading a simple recipe--all these things shape a child's learning.

Furthermore, language, experiences are also important when children are playing in their centers. The dialogues that teachers have with children expand his or her learning. If teachers are disciplining all the time and never really having conversations with children then children don't develop rich language experiences and similarly if parents don't communicate at home with students they don't develop the kinds of language behavior that expands their language and increases their knowledge of words, which as a result increases academic success. When teachers read stories and children are often listening to stories they develop a sense of story structure but children need lots of these experiences in order to understand them.

It is just like riding a bike, if you don't do it all the time you won't know how its done and you won't have the experiences you need in order to ride.

Teachers have to provide many opportunities for children to see them reading and writing but these reading and writing experiences have to be intentionally planned and teachers' have to know what they want to address and assess at the time of these experiences or they will amount to nothing. Below are lists of ideas to encourage more of these literacy experiences with preschoolers:

- Writing and reading recipes
- Using puppets to tell stories
- Write charts
- Writing a grocery list
- Taking dictation from a child
- Writing poems
- Reading charts in the preschool environment
- Listening to stories
- Observing types of print and fonts
- Writing on different types of paper

- Reading and writing a letter to a friend
- Creating greeting cards
- Copying a note
- Writing by drawing
- Pretend play with puppets
- Dramatic play area with friends
- Inventing spelling

These are just a few ideas and experiences to use with preschoolers on a daily basis. If teachers don't provide these literacy experiences daily, then don't expect the assessment to yield what you expect of children and to be anything higher than what you have put into it. As teachers, and directors of preschool centers, you have to really impact what students are learning and then provide rich opportunities.

Milestones of Preschoolers 3s, 4s and 5 year Olds

The developmental milestones to follow are characteristics of 3s, 4s and 5 year olds. These milestones should be considered when assessing children at various developmental levels to plan activities and create lessons that are appropriate for their development. Teachers already know that they have to be cognizant of the needs of all students by differentiating instruction to address the many learning styles of students.

In addition, educators also know that three, four and five year olds are exploring the world in developmentally different ways and to meet their needs. Teachers have to create learning environments that are productive and engaging for our young learners. Preschool teachers have to constantly reflect on what is developmentally appropriate for threes, fours and five year olds and plan appropriate and meaningful lessons that characterize what each age level can do and encourage students' progress by analyzing the data.

Characteristics of 3-Year Olds

Physical Development:

- Fine motor and gross motor skills are developing
- 3 year olds need lots of practice with using their hands: cutting, painting, gluing, writing, coloring, rolling a ball, playing with clay, fastening button, zipping, tying, finger painting and much more
- 3 year olds enjoy dancing, climbing, and running, jumping, throwing, catching, pulling and clapping their hands.
- 3 year olds love moving and their bodies really have to develop control over time.

Cognitive Development:

- 3 year olds can't distinguish between real and make believe
- They are visual, kinetic and tactile learners.
- 3 year olds like to ask questions: "Why are you doing that?" "Why does this work like that?" "Where are you going?" "Can I play with this?" "Why?"
- 3 year olds are eager to please.
- 3 year olds understand "smaller" and "larger"
- 3 year olds use words to describe space such as "back," "up," "outside," "in front of," "in back of," "over," and "next to."

Social/Emotional Development:

- 3 year olds have an egocentric behavior—it's all about "me" and "my."
- They are learning to share things and sharing is difficult (Teachers should have duplicate favorite toys in the classroom.)
- 3 year olds enjoy helping and responsibilities
- 3 year olds somewhat like to be independent i.e. "I can do it on my own."
- 3 year olds love to look at themselves.

Language Development:

- 3 year olds ask a lot of "why" questions
- They love to talk
- 3 year olds repeat words and phrases
- Sometime 3 year olds speech is not clear
- 3 year olds can recite simple rhymes and poems.

Characteristics of 4 year olds

Physical Development:
- 4 year olds fine motor and gross motor skills are developing.
- 4 year olds can write, cut, paste and glue objects
- 4 year olds can climb; ride a tricycle, balance, hop, skip and jump.
- They can throw and catch a ball.

Cognitive Development:

- 4 year olds have difficulty with real and make believe
- They can copy their names and other letters
- 4 year olds can count from 1-10 and higher
- 4 year olds can role play
- 4 year olds like to pretend
- They can pose a problem and find a solution
- 4 year olds are aware of 1 to 1 correspondent and patterns in their environment.

Social/Emotional Development:

- 4 year olds exhibit egocentric behavior
- 4 year olds can follow classroom rules when prompted
- They know how to share
- 4 year olds enjoy helping and responsibilities
- 4 year olds like to be independent
- 4 year olds plays well with at least one child
- They enjoy learning about how to take turns (board games are fun)
- 4 year olds can show empathy for others.

Language Development:

- 4 year olds ask questions about the world.
- 4 year olds love big words.
- 4 year olds can articulate wants and needs.
- They have an expanded vocabulary.
- 4 year olds can verbally dictate a story.
- They can conjure up prior knowledge and experiences from the past.

Characteristics of 5 years olds

Physical Development:

- 5 year olds fine motor skill are advanced
- They can balance well
- 5 year olds are good at catching, bouncing and throwing
- They can paste small and big objects
- They are good at cutting, gluing, writing and holding a pencil

Cognitive Development:

- 5 year olds can distinguish between real and make believe.
- Letters are more recognizable.
- They can ask "how," "what," and "why" questions.
- They can count to 50 and larger numbers.
- 5 year olds can name the days of the week.
- 5 year olds have a vocabulary of 2000 words or more.
- 5 year olds are beginning to identify letters in his/her name.

Social/Emotional Development:

- 5 year olds can maintain friendships with peers.
- 5 year olds use words to express feelings and emotions.
- 5 year olds know how to share.
- They should empathy for others.
- 5 year olds copy adult behavior.
- 5 year olds like helping and being responsible.
- They know how to take turns.
- 5 year olds like being independent.

Language Development:

- 5 year olds can retell a story in their own words.
- 5 year olds are beginning to ask how to spell words.
- 5 year olds have expanded oral language.
- They can express wants and needs.

- 5 year olds can read stories on his/her own.
- 5 year olds can explain why something happens.

In summary, when assessing preschoolers at different age levels it is important to examine and understand their developmental levels and know exactly what they can do. Often, teachers make the mistake of creating activities that young children don't understand because they are not ready for it or the activity is way beyond their level of understanding. Directors of preschool centers or buildings should also have a good deal of knowledge about developmental levels especially if they are going to coach and evaluate teachers on their lessons and activities in the classroom.

Getting Ready for Assessment Questions to Think About

When getting ready for assessment here are some questions and ideas to think about:

1. Decide how you are going to organize the information
2. Think about the collection of data and what you are looking for.
3. Create a timeline in which you will tell teachers to start and end.
4. Think about what the documentation will look like.
5. Remember that teachers need to think about the domains: Physical, Cognitive, Social/Emotional and Language of children.
6. Think about the accessibility of the information and where is it going to be stored for you the director to access it.
7. As the director, when will you conduct meetings to discuss the information?
8. How will you decide if progress is being made and who will decide the next steps to take.

9. Who will participate in your assessment meetings and what will the agenda look like over a period of time.
10. How will the teachers share the information with parents?
11. How can you make assessment an on-going process of looking and sharing data with teachers and parents?

Links to Important Websites for Directors

Education Resources Information Center (ERIC)
www.eric.ed.gov

Sage research methods online: Assessment for Effective Intervention
www.sagepub.com

Children, Youth and Families: Education & Research Network: Practical Research-based information from the Nation's Leading Universities
www.cyfernet.org

The Consumer Product Safety Commissions: Playground Safety Publications
www.cpsc.gov

Natural Learning Initiative
www.naturalearning.org

U.S. Environmental Protection Agency
www.epa.gov

National Association of School Psychologists
www.nasponline.org

Environment Rating Scales
www.fpg.unc.edu/

Preschool Education
www.preschooleducation.com

Preschool Special Education
www.p12.nysed.gov

The PE Central: The Premier Website for Health & Physical Education
www.pecentral.org

Science Direct
www.sciencedirect.com

ies National Center for Education Evaluation and Regional Assistance
www.ies.ed.gov

BMC Public Health (Free registration and search Preschools)
www.biomedcentral.com

Ablenet: Play & Learn: A Preschool Curriculum for Children of All Abilities
www.ablenetinc.com

The National Association for the Education of Young Children (naeyc)
www.naeyc.org

Circle of Inclusion
www.circleofinclusion.org

Child Development Media
www.childdevelopmentmedia.com

Seed of Life Center for Early Learning & Preschool, LLC
www.seedoflifellc.com

Spectronics
www.spectronicsinoz.com

LD Online
www.LDOnline.org

Teachingpoint
www.teaching-point.net

Sites for Teachers
www.sitesforteachers.com

Kid Source
www.kidsource.com

Books on Assessment

Data-Based Decision Making, Second Edition, National Association of Elementary School Principals

Data Analysis: for Continuous School Improvement
Victoria L. Bernhardt, Ph.D.

Psychoeducation Assessment of Preschool Children, 4th
Bruce A. Bracben, Richard J. Nagle.

Early Language and Literacy Classroom Observation Tool
Miriam W. Smith, Ed.D

Seven Strategies of Assessment for Learning - 10 Books (Assessment Training Institute, Inc.) [Misc. Sup
Jan Chappuis, Chris Harrison, Clare Lee, Bethan Marshall

Assessment for Learning: Putting it into Practice
Paul Black, Dylan William, Open University Press

Ahead of the Curve: The Power of Assessment to Transform Teaching and Learning
Larry Ainsworth, Lisa Almeida , Anne Davies, Richard DuFour , Linda Gregg, Thomas Guskey , Robert Marzano , Ken O'Connor, Rick Stiggins, Stephen White, Dylan Wiliam, Douglas Reeves

Professional Learning Communities at Work: Best Practices for Enhancing Student Achievement
Richard Dufour, Robert Eaker

Classroom Assessment for Student Learning: Doing it Right - Using it Well
Richard J. Stiggins, Judith A. Arter, Jan Chappuis, Stephen Chappuis

Assessment for Learning: An Action Guide for School Leaders (2nd Edition)
Stephen Chappuis, Carol Commodore, Richard J. Stiggins

References

Airasian, P.W. (1994). Classroom assessment. New York, NY:McGraw-Hill, Inc.

Ardovino, J., Hollingsworth,J., & Ybarra,S. (2000).

Aschbacher, P.R., Koency,G., & Schacter J. (1995). Los Angles Learning Center alternative assessment guidebook: Los Angeles, CA: National Center for Research on Evaluation, Standards, and Student Testing (CRESST)

Arter,J., & The Classroom Assessment Team, Laboratory Network Program. (1998). Improving classroom assessment: A toolkit for professional developers: Alternative Assessment. Aurora, CO:MCREL

Berhardt, Victoria L., Ph.D., (1998) Data Analysis: for Continuous School Improvement (p.56-70)

Diane Trister Dodge, Laura J. Colker, and Cate Heroman, (2002) Creative Curriculum for Preschool (p. 40-45)

Harms, Thelma, Clifford M. Richard and Cryer, Debby, (2004) Early Childhood Environment Rating Scale, Revised Edition (p. 33-39)

Teaching Strategies, (2006) The Creative Curriculum for Preschool Implementation Checklist, (p.40-43)

Appendix

Interventions
www.cpdusu.org/projects/spies/

SPIES for Parents and Strategies for Preschool Intervention in Everyday Settings (SPIES)

SPIES for Parents is a web based curriculum built to help caregivers learn to use daily activities to teach preschool children. Video clips and text suggest ways to talk to children and give them help during everyday routines in order to help their development and learning.

Strategies for Preschool Intervention in Everyday Settings (SPIES)
www.spiesforparents.cpd.usu.edu/Start.htm includes other information for parents such as: links to other helpful websites - strategies that teachers use in preschool classrooms - a language development program, Kid Talk, by authors at Vanderbilt University

Family First Intervention
http://familyfirstintervention.com
A website that offer a host of programs for families in need of specific interventions and adult services. Get services for treatment of health issues: autism, physical disabilities, alcoholism and drug addition, plan parenthood issues and much more.

NJ Health Link
http://www.state.nj.us/njhealthlink

The website offers links to various services for families and children and anyone in need of interventions: treatment and screening for specific diseases, community health centers, designated screening centers, early intervention system, family centered care services and emergency resources hotlines.

New Jersey Inclusive Child Care Project
http://www.spannj.org

New Jersey Resources: Government Agencies

New Jersey Developmental Disabilities Council Education Subcommittee P.O. Box 700 20 West State Street, 7th Floor Trenton, NJ 08625-0700 Susan Richmond (609) 292-3745 Fax: (609) 292-7114

Special Child Health Services Case Management Units Pauline Lisciotto (609) 777-7778

New Jersey Department of Health and Senior Services – Early Intervention Services P.O. Box 364 Trenton, NJ 08625-0364 Terry L. Harrison, Part C Coordinator (609) 777-7734 Fax: (609) 292-0296

New Jersey Department of Education Office of Special Education Programs Preschool Coordinator: Barbara Tkach (609) 984-4950

New Jersey Department of Education Learning Resource Centers (LRCs)

LRC North 240 So. Harrison Street, 6th Floor, East Orange, NJ 07018 Preschool Consultant: Paquita Roberts (973) 414-4491

LRC North Satellite 322 American Road, Morris Plains, NJ 07950 Preschool Consultant: Paquita Roberts (973) 414-4491

LRC Central 1 Crest Way, Aberdeen, NJ 07747 Preschool Consultant: Sue Leonard (732) 441-0460

LRC South 606 Delsea Drive, Sewell, NJ 08080 Preschool Consultant: Claire Punda (609) 582-7000 x155

New Jersey Resource and Referral Agencies North Jersey 4 C's 101 Oliver Street Paterson, NJ 07501 Mary Ann Mirko, Executive Director (973) 684-1904 Fax: (973) 684-0468

New Jersey's Special Needs Child Care Project Department of Human Services Office of Early Care and Education P.O. Box 700 Trenton, NJ 08625 Jane Voorhees (609) 292-8444 Fax: (609) 292-1903 E-mail: jvoorhees@dhs.state.nj.us

New Jersey Resources: Non-Profit Agencies

Family Support Center

Lions Head Office Park 35 Beaverson Blvd, Suite 8A, Brick, NJ 08723 (800) FSC-NJ10 (732) 262-8020 Fax: (732) 262-7805

Family Voices of New Jersey

c/o Statewide Parent Advocacy Network (SPAN) 35 Halsey Street, 4th Floor, Newark, NJ 07102 Lauren Agoratus: (609) 584-5779 (Phone & Fax) Louise McIntosh: (908) 277-2883 Fax: (908) 277-1969

NJ Inclusive Child Care Project (NJICCP)

Statewide Parent Advocacy Network (SPAN) 35 Halsey Street, 4th Floor, Newark, NJ 07102 Contact: Susan Merrill, Project Director (973) 642-8100 x108 (800) 654-SPAN x108 Fax: (973) 642-3766

New Jersey Head Start Association

1440 Pennington Road, Trenton, NJ 08818 Audrey Fletcher: (609) 771-8401 Fax: (609) 771-8405

New Jersey Statewide Parent to Parent c/o Statewide Parent Advocacy Network (SPAN) 35 Halsey Street, 4th Floor, Newark, NJ 07102 Malia Corde, Project Coordinator: (800) 654-7726 (800) 372-6510 for matches Statewide Parent Advocacy Network is a network of parents supporting families of children with developmental delays, disabilities, or other special health needs. Provides one-to-one matches of families who have similar needs and experiences.

Quality Improvement Center for Disabilities New York University School of Education 726 Broadway, 5th Floor, New York, NY 10003-9580 Contact: Barbara Schwartz (800) 533-1498 (212) 998-5528 Fax: (212) 995-4562

Technical assistance and support to NJ Head Start agencies regarding inclusion of young children with disabilities.

Special Olympics New Jersey 201 Rockingham Row, Princeton, NJ 08540 Contact: Nancy Vitalone (800) 336-6576x19 (609) 734-8400 Fax: (609) 734-0911

Provides information, training and technical assistance regarding inclusion of children and youth with disabilities in recreation activities.

Statewide Parent Advocacy Network of New Jersey, Inc. (SPAN) 35 Halsey Street, 4th Floor, Newark, NJ 07102 Contact: Diana Autin, Executive Director (973) 642-8100 (800) 654-SPAN Fax: (973) 642-8080 www.spannj.org Inclusion ToolKit for Parents, Teachers and Administrators.

Cerebral Palsy of New Jersey 354 South Broad Street, Trenton, NJ 08608 (888)-322-1918 TTY: (609) 392-7044 Fax: (609) 392-3505

This is a great resource in solving problems with education, employment, assistive technology, advocacy, housing, the ADA, and other concerns for people with all types of disabilities.

University-Affiliated Program of New Jersey (Elizabeth Boggs Center) 335 George Street, P.O. Box 2688 New Brunswick, NJ 08903-2688 Karen Melzer: (732) 235-9300 Fax: (732) 235-9330

INCLUSION RESOURCES FOR PROFESSIONALS AND FAMILIES

National Resources

ADA Information (800) 514-0301 (voice) (800) 514-0383 (TDD)

Provides answers to general and technical questions Monday-Friday 10am-6pm, except Thursdays when hours are 1pm-6pm EST. Regulations and other free materials available for mail delivery 24 hours a day.

Administration for Children & Families – Child Care Bureau: Inclusion Technical Assistance Region II (includes New Jersey) 26 Federal Plaza, Room 4114 New York, NY 10278 Souvonia Taylor (212) 264-2667 Fax: (212) 264-4881

Association for Supervision and Curriculum Development (ASCD) 1703 N. Beauregard Street Alexandria, VA 22311-1714 (800) 933-2723 Fax: (703) 575-5400

The Children's Foundation 725 15th Street NW, #505 Washington, DC 20005 (202) 347-3300 Fax: (202) 347-3382 www.childrensfoundation.net

The Foundation produced a videotape and resource directory for working with infants and toddlers with disabilities in family child care, with useful information applicable across ages and settings.

Council for Exceptional Children - Division for Early Childhood 1110 North Glebe Road, Suite 300 Arlington, VA 22201 (888) 232-7733 Fax: (703) 264-9494 www.cec.sped.org

Disability Resources, Inc. 4 Glatter Lane Centerreach, NY 11720 Julie Klauber (631) 585-0290 (phone & fax) www.disabilityresources.org

ERIC Clearinghouse on Elementary and Early Childhood Education University of Illinois Children's Research Center 51 Gerty Drive Champaign, IL 61820-7469 (800) 583-4135 (217) 333-1386 Fax: (217) 333-3767 www.ericeece.org

Head Start Information and Publication Center 1133 15th Street, NW, Suite 45D Washington, DC 20005 (202) 639-4465 Fax: (202) 737-1151 www.acf.dhhs.gov

Head Start Resource Access Project Education Development Center, Inc. 55 Chapel Street Newton, MA 02458 Contact: Philip Printz (617) 969-7100 Fax: (617) 244-3609 www.EDC.org.

Inclusion Press International 24 Thome Crescent Toronto, ON, Canada M6H 2S5 (416) 658-5363 Fax: (416) 658-5067 www.inclusion.com

Inclusion Press is a small independent press that produces resources about full inclusion in school, work, and community.

Kids Together, Inc.: Information for Children and Adults with Disabilities P.O. Box 574 Quakertown, PA 18951 (800) 879-2301 http://www.kidstogether.org/inc.htm

National Association of Child Care Resource and Referral Agencies 1319 F Street NW Suite 810 Washington, DC 20004-1106 (202) 393-5501 Fax: (202)-393-1109

National Association for the Education of Young Children 1509 Sixteenth Street NW Washington, DC 20036 Pat Spahr, Info Development Dir, x11630 (800) 424-2460 (202) 232-8777 Fax: (202) 328-1846 www.naeyc.org

National Center for Educational Restructuring and Inclusion CUNY Grad Center 365 Fifth Avenue New York, NY 10016 Alan Gartner or Dorothy Kerzner Lipsky (212) 817-2090 Fax: (212) 817-1607

National Child Care Information Center (NCCIC) 243 Church Street NW, 2nd Floor Vienna, VA 22180 (800) 616-2242 Fax: (800) 716-2242 www.nccic.org Barbara Scott, New Jersey State TA Specialist (609) 758-5646 Fax: (609) 758-4660 E-mail: bscott@nccic.org

National Early Childhood Technical Assistance System (NEC*TAS) 500 Bank of America Plaza 137 East Franklin Street Chapel Hill, NC 27514 Contact: Cathy Festa (919) 962-2001 Fax: (919) 966-7463 www.nectas.unc.edu

National Education Association 1201 Sixteenth Street NW Washington, DC 20036 (202) 833-4000 Fax: (202) 822-7206 www.nea.org

National Information Center for Children and Youth with Disabilities (NICHCY) P.O. Box 1492 Washington, D.C. 20013-1492 (800) 695-0285 Fax: (202) 884-8441 www.nichcy.org

Specializes in providing information and support to parents of children with disabilities and to those who work with these families.

National Institute on Disability and Rehabilitation Research ADA Regional Technical Assistance Centers/ U.S. Department of Education 3100 Clarendon Blvd. Arlington, VA 22201 (703) 525-3268 (800) 949-4232 Fax: (703) 525-3585

National Institute on Out-of-School Time Wellesley College Center for Research on Women 106 Central Street Wellesley, MA 02481 (781) 283-2547 Fax (781) 283-3657 www.niost.org

National Parent Network on Disabilities 1130 Seventeenth Street NW, Suite 400 Washington, D.C. 20036 Pat Smith, Executive Director (202) 463-2299 E-mail: Pmcglsmith@aol.com www.npnd.org

Publications: All Children Belong training materials for awareness, implementation of inclusion for one student, and implementation of inclusion throughout a school and district.

PEAK Parent Center 611 North Weber Street, #200 Colorado Springs, CO 80903 (800) 284-0251 (719) 531-9400 Fax: (719) 531-9452 Barbara Buswell

Publications: Building Integration with the IEP (1989); Breaking Ground: Ten Families Building Opportunities Through Integration (1989); Discover the Possibilities: A Curriculum for Teaching Parents About Integration (1988); Connecting Students: A Guide to Thoughtful Friendship Facilitation for Educators and Families (1992); Opening Doors: Strategies for Including All Students in Regular Education (1991)

Regional Resource and Federal Centers Network Federal Resource Center for Special Education 1875 Connecticut Avenue NW, Suite 900 Washington, D.C. 20009 (202) 884-8215 Fax: (202) 884-8443 http://www.dssc.org/frc/

Offers tools and strategies that identify appropriate solutions for effective education and human services delivery systems, serving all states and outlying jurisdictions. Specifically funded to assist state education agencies in improving education programs, practices, and policies that affect children and youth with disabilities.

School and Community Inclusion Project University of Utah 1705 East Campus Center Drive, Room 221 Salt Lake City, UT 84112 (801) 585-3189 Fax (801) 585-7291 Contact: Camille McQuivey E-mail: mcquiv_c@ed.utah.edu http://www.gse.utah.edu/sped/inclusn.htm

TASH: The Association for Persons with Severe Handicaps 29 West Susquehanna Avenue, Suite 210 Baltimore, MD 21204 (410) 828-8274 Fax: (410) 828-6706 TDD (410) 828-1306 E-mail: info@tash.org www.tash.org

National Childcare Program The Children's Foundation 725 Fifteenth Street NW, Suite 505 Washington, D.C. 20005-2109 (202) 347-3300 Fax: (202) 347-3382 Kay Hollestelle

Publications: **"Yes, You Can Do It! Caring for Infants and Toddlers with Disabilities in Family Child Care"** video and Annotated Resource Directory. Trains family childcare providers who are caring for children with disabilities to be mentors for less experienced providers who would like to care for children with special needs.

Zero to Three: National Center for Clinical Infant Programs
200 M Street NW, Suite 200 Washington, D.C. 20036-3307 (202) 638-1144 Fax: (202) 638-0851 www.zerotothree.org

INCLUSION RESOURCES FOR PROFESSIONALS AND FAMILIES Compiled by Orah Raia and E. Fine

ABCs of Inclusion Manual
http://www.projectchoices.org/abcs.htm

This is a manual that can be downloaded. Topics include collaboration, related services, IEPs and supports, peer interactions, assessment and transition.

ADA Home Page on the Internet
www.usdoj.gov/crt/ada/adahom1.htm

The Department of Justice's ADA Home Page provides free information including technical assistance materials, enforcement information including settlement agreements, links to other Federal agencies, and updates on new and pending ADA requirements.

Axis Disability Rights Website www.normemma.com

Operated by Norman Kunc and Emma Van der Klift of Axis Consultation & Training, Ltd. and dedicated to the distribution of information concerning disability rights.

The Book on Inclusive Education: Inclusion, School as a CaringCommunity
www.quasar.ualberta.ca/ddc/inclusion/index/html

Includes a handbook on inclusion with field notes and other resources (materials/reprints from important inclusion books); interviews with 100 teachers who have had successful inclusion experiences.

Centre for Studies on Inclusive Education
http://inclusion.uwe.ac.uk/csie/csiehome.htm

This is a British independent educational charity providing information and advice about inclusive education and related issues. Also contains information on international perspectives regarding inclusion.

Circle of Inclusion Outreach Training Project
http://circleofinclusion.org/

Designed to address the challenges and issues of inclusive program development for children with severe, multiple disabilities. Offers demonstrations of and information about the effective practices of inclusive educational programs for children from birth through age eight.

Council for Exceptional Children www.cec.sped.org

Provides resources for professionals who work with children with disabilities.

Early Childhood Research Institute on Inclusion
www.fpg.unc.edu/~ecrii

This is a five-year national research project funded by the U.S. Department of Education to study the inclusion of preschool children with disabilities in typical preschool, day care and community settings.

Family Education Network www.familyeducation.com

Includes a special needs section and an eight part series about a family's experience with inclusion.

Family Village Inclusion Page
www.familyvillage.wisc.edu/education/inclusion.html

Provides information on "who to contact," on-line articles/newsletters, recommended reading, research, videos, conferences, and additional links.

Inclusion Press www.inclusion.com This website contains many articles and resources on inclusion, circle of friends, MAPS and the PATH process

Integrating Children with Disabilities into Preschool
www.kidsource.com/kidsource/content/preschool.disabilities.html

Kids Together, Inc. Inclusion Page
www.kidstogether.org/inc.htm Nonprofit organization co-founded by parents and organized by volunteers designed to promote inclusive communities where all people belong. This site contains a variety of helpful information and resources on inclusion.

National Center to Improve Practices in Special Education Through Technology, Media and Materials
http://www2.edc.org/FSC .

National Information Center for Children and Youth with Disabilities (NICHCY) www.nichcy.org

Contains many resources, digests, and articles on disability issues.

Preschool Inclusion Connection www.truecoaching.com/pic

Free preschool inclusion monthly newsletter and thematic lessons, inclusion activities and parent page.

Project MESH: The MESH Manual for Inclusive Schools
www.newhorizons.org/spneeds_meshman.html

The Renaissance Group: Inclusive Education Web Site
www.uni.edu/coe/inclusion/

Special Education Resources on the Internet
www.hood.edu/seri/serihome.htm

Exceptional Children Magazine www.cec.sped.org

Made in the USA
Lexington, KY
26 September 2014